Ingo Arndt | Fritz Jantschke

MONKEYS AND APES

IN THE WILD

WITH A FOREWORD BY FRANS DE WAAL

PAPADAKIS

First published in Great Britain in 2008 by
Papadakis Publisher
An imprint of New Architecture Group Ltd.

PAPADAKIS

Head office:
Kimber, Winterbourne, Berkshire RG20 8AN

Design Studio & Retail:
Studio 11 Shepherd Market, Mayfair, London W1J 7PG

Exhibition Gallery:
Monkey Island, Bray-on-Thames, Berkshire, SL6 4EE

Tel. +44 (0)20 78 23 23 23
info@papadakis.net
www.papadakis.net

A book from the partners
FREDERKING & THALER and GEO

Copyright © 2007
Frederking & Thaler Verlag GmbH, München
www.frederking-thaler.de

Photos, introduction and captions:
Ingo Arndt, www.ingoarndt.com
The images in this book have not been digitally manipulated
or enhanced. All the images were taken in the wild except
the following, which were taken in zoos only in order
to complete the "Other Primates" chapter at the end:
ring-tailed lemurs (pp. 206, 207), mandrill (p. 213), Barbary
macaques (pp. 214, 215), white-faced saki (p. 220).

Text: Dr. Fritz Jantschke, Laubach
With a foreword by Dr. Frans B. M. de Waal

Layout: Wunderamt, Munich

Jacket Design: Alexandra Papadakis

Production: Verlagsservice Rau, Munich

Reproduction: Reproline Genceller, Munich

English edition © Papadakis Publisher

English translation: Matthiesen, Edinburgh

Senior editor English edition: Alexandra Papadakis

Editor: Kevin White for bookwise GmbH, Munich

Printed in China

ISBN 978-1901092-912

A CIP catalogue of this book is available from the British Library.

CONTENTS

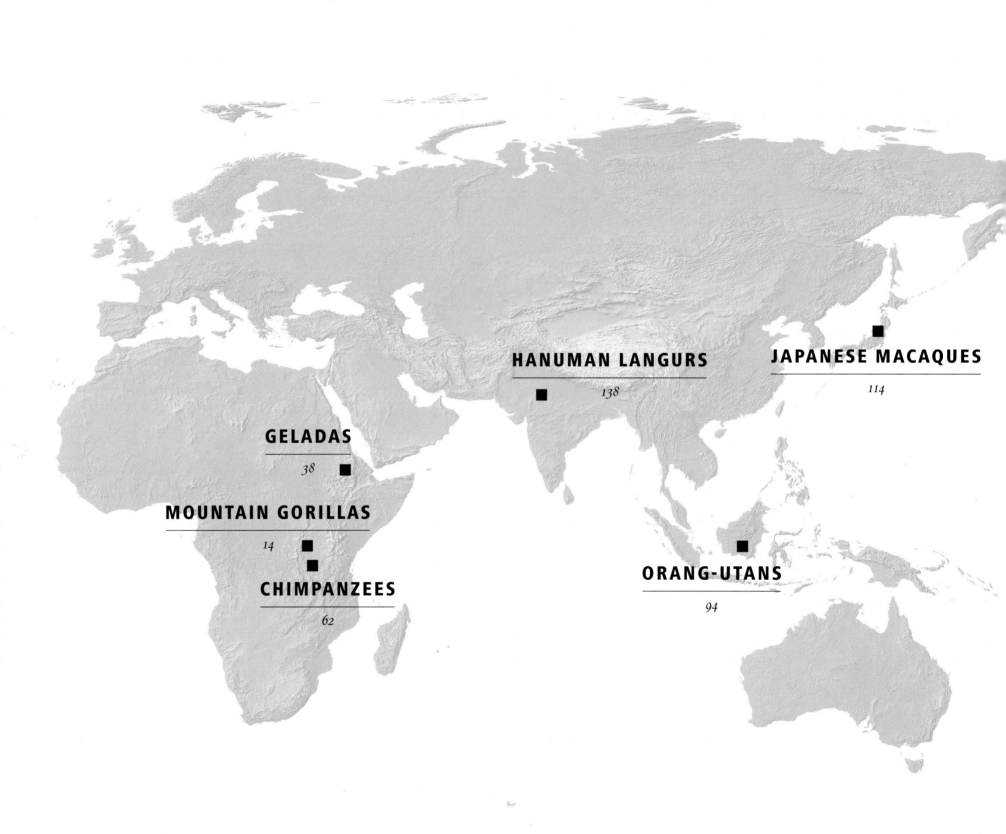

Foreword

FRANS DE WAAL

I once took part in an expert panel on the subject of apes – it included renowned field researchers, laboratory scientists and people like me who were somewhere in between – and a poignant question was raised: which moments in our careers did we regard as pivotal? Each of us told the story of the first time we made personal eye contact with an ape. It had been the moment that changed our lives and inspired us to learn more about these creatures, to which we all felt an obvious connection. The eyes of an ape are something truly extraordinary, and no other encounters with animals can compare with the exchange of glances with an ape, despite the fact that many other animals have eyes that face forward. Apes look at us with the same curiosity, the same contemplation and the same intense emotion that humans express in their faces. Compared to the eyes of an ape, the eyes of an owl, for example, appear "empty." To us, apes and humans are very much alike.

Many people misinterpret the correlation between evolution and human dignity as a zero-sum game – as if all arguments for one are also arguments against the other. I personally would like the debate on evolution to be focused more on the beauty of the concept and less on where humans fit into it. For me the effect has been quite the opposite: the more I learn about our origins and how much we have in common with other living beings, the more comfortable I feel being placed in this structure. The connection is so clear to me that even Darwin's statement that humans are descendants of apes falls short of expressing the matter. We are not just descended from them. We are apes.

Allegedly, Carl Linnaeus originally placed humans in the separate genus *Homo* only in order to avoid trouble with the Vatican. He already knew how weak the arguments for a separate category were. Indeed, with DNA that is 98.5 per cent identical to that of chimpanzees and baboons, we certainly don't have much reason to feel that we are something special. Of course, the chimpanzee that most people are familiar with – a dressed-up, circus animal doing tricks for us in Hollywood films – does not inspire much of a feeling of connection. It is we who put apes into these humiliating costumes and ridiculous situations, seemingly in a vain attempt to keep our distance from them. Yet the apes I know are different. When left alone, they are incredibly dignified, intelligent and endearing. The photographs here capture apes in their natural setting, and ironically it is here that they appear much more human than when we so crudely dictate their behaviour. But this is not only true for apes – which includes chimps, orang-utans and gorillas – but also for our more distant relatives, the monkeys. They are all primates, and the similarities are obvious!

The order primates contains some 200 species, making it difficult to fully portray their diversity in just one volume. This book does, however, offer a cross-section of all primates and brings a number of these wonderful species closer to us. Some of them are under a serious threat of extinction and it should be our ambition to raise awareness of this threat and attempt to reverse this unfortunate trend.

These animals are not only beautiful to watch, but they can also teach us so much about our own behaviour which, after all, was shaped by their behaviour, the behaviour of our primate ancestors.

We can all recognize the common bond of evolution that connects us. "There is grandeur in this view of life," noted Darwin in his groundbreaking work, "The Origin of the Species" and it is obvious that he saw precisely those bonds that you can now discover in abundance in this breathtaking book.

Introduction

INGO ARNDT

I photographed monkeys in the wild for the first time in the winter of 1994/95, when I spent six weeks with the Hanuman langurs in the Thar Desert of Northwest India. Every day I travelled with these monkeys and, luckily for me, they quickly accepted me as a harmless addition to their environment. They eventually began to trust me and I was able to make many unexpected observations. During longer resting periods, the langurs even fell asleep just a few metres away – to me an unmistakable sign of trust and a great compliment. Other times I witnessed bloody battles between neighbouring groups including strategic attacks to steal females, and fights for new feeding grounds. The most fascinating element of this first journey to see the Hanuman langurs, however, was the diversity of behaviour that these monkeys exhibited, made all the more striking by the obvious similarities to us humans. It was then that I decided to continue photographing other monkeys and apes, and a long-term project was born.

My expeditions to observe the various primates of the world were rife with both luck and disappointment. It took three separate journeys, for example, before I finally got the pictures of mountain gorillas that I wanted. The first two trips to Uganda and Rwanda had ended in vain and it was only during my third visit to the Virunga Mountains in Rwanda that I was able to photograph the majestic creatures as I had envisaged them. Some time later, a BBC TV documentary inspired me to travel to the mountains of Ethiopia in search of the rarely photographed geladas. Unfortunately, the turmoil in that war-torn country made this journey impossible for several years. When visiting orang-utans in the jungles of Borneo I lived on a small wooden boat and a local guide took me on remote blackwater rivers to observe the last survivors of this glorious ape species. Despite their considerable size, however,

PAGE 3
Large mammals, a category into which most species of monkeys and apes fall, need a lot of space to live. But an insatiable human need for ever more land has destroyed natural habitats around the globe. Many species, including the mountain gorilla have only relatively small areas left to take refuge from encroaching civilization. They must now be content with roaming the last remaining forests on the slopes of the Virunga volcanoes.

During my expeditions I often lived in rather unconventional lodgings. When I visited the chimpanzees of Gombe, for example, a hut on the shores of Lake Tanganyika was my home for several weeks. All windows and doors were protected by a massive grid of wires against roaming olive baboons that would otherwise have immediately raided my supply of bananas and vegetables.

the orang-utans consistently managed to remain hidden in the dense rainforest. Our expedition to the Amazon basin was also a huge challenge, where day after day I wandered for hours through dense rainforests and palm swamps before I finally found a group of red uakaris. The reward for these efforts: the first photo documentary ever of these very strange, rare monkeys.

All of these expeditions required meticulous planning from my native Germany. It was essential, and often difficult, to establish contacts with local authorities and scientists in some of the most remote regions of the world, and comprehensive travel plans and detailed packing lists were needed. I then checked everything obsessively for completeness because once you are out in the field it is often impossible to obtain things that you have forgotten. Ultimately, however, the most challenging element of these trips proved to be the diverse habitats themselves.

Extended treks were an everyday routine and I often had to crawl for hours through thick undergrowth. Beyond that, nasty insects, hot, humid climates or freezing weather – depending on the region – hampered our progress. Without the support of local guides and porters many of my projects would certainly have been destined for failure. Local scientists were elemental in providing me with valuable data from years of painstaking field research, and even occasionally accompanied me in the field. My camera equipment also had to withstand extreme conditions: in the Japanese Alps the batteries for my camera and flash failed at minus 20°C (-4°F); in a Costa Rican jungle my lenses filled with water; and in the Indian desert adolescent Hanuman langurs ransacked an unguarded pack with my photo gear. I often chose the freedom of a tent or a hammock over the often uninviting accommodation. But all of these inconveniences faded during the fascinating encounters I had. A male mountain gorilla, a mature silverback, looked straight into my eyes from only a few metres away and made me freeze with respect. Geladas in Ethiopia perched easily and majestically on a promontory 1,500 metres above the valley floor – an impressive view and no sign of vertigo! A curious baby chimpanzee looked at me with the large, fascinated eyes of a child, calling to mind how strikingly similar we primates really are. I wouldn't trade a single moment of all these experiences.

As a wildlife photographer, I can hardly imagine anything more beautiful than observing apes and monkeys in their natural environment, and capturing them through the lens of my camera. I knew there would be extraordinary moments for outstanding pictures during the many weeks of my journeys, and in that sense time was indeed on my side. My primary goal was to capture the personality of each individual animal, the character of each species, and to use intimate insights to tell stories about their everyday lives.

This book does not claim to be comprehensive or complete, and it is not meant as a textbook. It is simply the result of more than ten years of photos taken on twelve different journeys. Many monkey and – in particular – all ape species are endangered today. To be sure, environmentalists have long campaigned and worked for their protection, but it will take a lot more to save these animals from extinction in the long run. The problems that need to be solved are complex. For me the first step on the way to supporting these threatened species is to awaken interest and enthusiasm for them. My greatest wish is that this book will make at least a small contribution to that noble effort.

Africa

GELADAS

MOUNTAIN GORILLAS

CHIMPANZEES

MOUNTAIN GORILLAS

THE GENTLE GIANTS

PAGE 15

I met Kwakane on the very first day of my third visit to the mountain gorillas *(Gorilla beringei)*. He appeared suddenly in the dense undergrowth just a few steps away from me. While the enormous silverback sized me up with his piercing eyes I lifted the camera very carefully. I could hardly bring myself to press the shutter release.

PAGE 16/17

At 4,507 metres Karisimbi is the highest mountain in the Virunga region, the homeland of the last mountain gorillas. In some seasons, impressive cloud formations develop over its summit. One morning, just after sunrise, this cloud settled on the extinct volcano.

After extensive rainfall, wafts of mist rise from the forests in the Virunga Mountains. This pristine territory is the habitat of the last mountain gorillas.

Everyone who has encountered mountain gorillas in their natural habitat has experienced this: after trekking for hours through the humid, steep mountain rainforests, you suddenly hear grunts and snorts from the dense bamboo undergrowth just a few metres away. Then comes the powerful drumming sound of a mighty "silverback" pounding his chest. It is an impressive sight that will immediately command respect for the incredible strength of these great apes. Indeed, similar encounters may well have been behind the horror stories John Speke, discoverer of the sources of the Nile, heard from Rwandan King Rumanika in 1860. That Central African monarch told of colossal ape monsters living in the Virunga Mountains who stole women from villages and crushed them to death in frenzies of lust. Ignorance, exaggeration and fantasy eventually transformed the gorillas into fearsome beasts. It wasn't until 1901 that a German captain, Robert von Beringe, at last managed to track and kill a couple of these "ape monsters" and reveal their true identity.

Since the 1980s, tourists have been able to observe these creatures at several sites in Rwanda, Uganda and Congo. The African scouts who guide visitor groups are experts on the behaviour of these apes, and can accurately judge the mock attacks of gorilla males when they begin their territorial displays. They can even speak to the angry apes to calm them down. Although gorillas may menacingly tear up a few bunches of grass or bamboo, they usually calm down quickly and return to their groups. In fact, this display behaviour typically has no serious impetus, but it enhances the reputation of the gorilla male within his troop. At an age of approximately twelve to fifteen years, the backs of the male gorillas slowly turn white and they become true "silverbacks." This is the phase when a fully grown male begins forming his own

harem – on average five females plus their offspring. Only rarely does the dominant male accept another silverback in his realm and the other males in the troop are often sons of the "monarch" who will eventually take over the troop when the father dies. Unlike other apes, gorilla males do not force females to remain in the harem. The females, even during chance encounters in the forest, often decide for themselves where their loyalty lies. They are also always the ones to leave the troop when they reach sexual maturity, a move that prevents incest within a clan.

Serious fights among gorillas are rare, but if two groups meet it can lead to heavy combat between the males, who occasionally seriously wound or even kill each other with their large canine teeth. Within their groups, mountain gorillas are actually quite peaceful and the role of harem leader is undisputed. He is the centre of all social activities, which consist mainly of mutual grooming among males and females. The females, for their part, treat each other quite neutrally, with no obvious ranking among them. And why should they compete? There is plenty of food available for these strict vegetarians, who eat mainly leaves, stalks and shoots.

Adult males weigh up to 270 kilograms and females up to 100 kilograms. Because of their weight they do not climb trees as much as other apes, preferring to spend most of the time on the ground. There are currently only 600 or 700 mountain gorillas left in Africa, and they are strictly protected in the Virunga Mountains. At present the closely-related lowland gorillas are more abundant, but they are becoming increasingly threatened: the flesh of these "gentle giants" ends up all too often as "bush meat" in the big cities.

We hiked for three hours from camp before encountering our first mountain gorillas, but a deep, impassable canyon separated us from them. The group was somewhat nervous and began making its way up the ridge individually rather than as a unit. My guide told me it was likely that they had just had an altercation with a neighbouring troop. Despite her size, the fully grown female in the lower right of the picture was difficult to spot from this distance in the dense vegetation.

PAGE 22/23
A mountain gorilla baby looks at me with wide, fascinated eyes. I took more than 30 shots of this adorable creature. Despite having a tripod and ultrasensitive film, the light was so bad that I thought they would all be blurred. Fortunately, this one came out fully in focus.

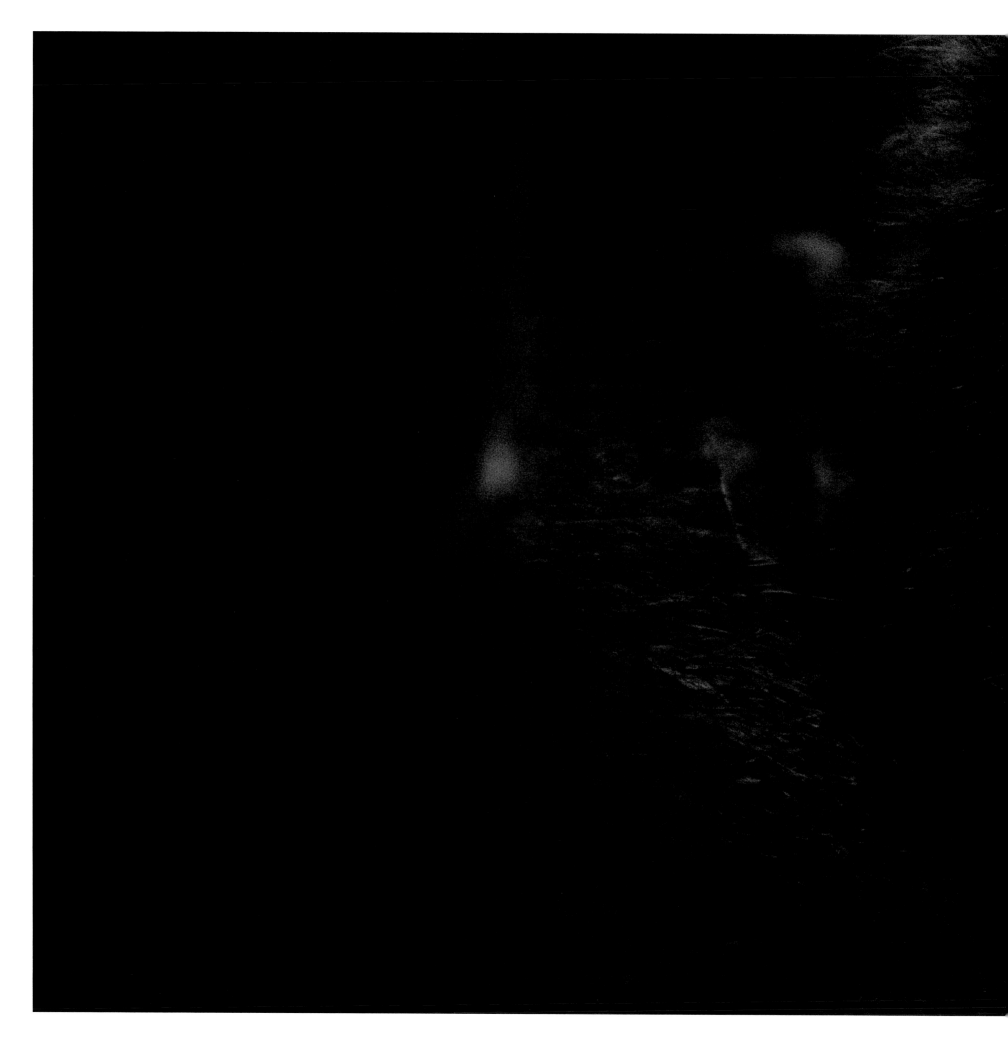

Who is really observing whom? While the group was resting, this not quite fully grown mountain gorilla played a game of "hide and seek" with me. Whenever I focused my camera on him, he hid his face behind the leaves. When I lowered my camera, he lifted his head again. This went on for a while until we finally both made eye contact at the same time.

Young mountain gorillas use their long resting periods for hours of frolicking and romping around. They don't seem to care much about the size of their playmates either. Even companions ten times their own weight are given no respect in these playful moments, as seen here where the little one seems to have the upper hand.

When the alpha male of a gorilla troop arrives on the scene, the other members tend to gather humbly together out of respect for their leader. Only the smallest ones are unimpressed by the show of power – they know the silverback is tolerant of his offspring.

When humans are nearby, mountain gorilla females prefer to remain in the background when breastfeeding their babies. After several visits, however, I was fortunate enough to catch a young gorilla feeding at its mother's breast just a few metres away.

Outside the national park, mountain gorillas peel the bark off eucalyptus trees to suck sap out of the trunk. Apes are obviously quite flexible when it comes to new sources of nutrition – eucalyptus are not native to these jungles, having spread around the world from Australia. One could ask oneself if the eucalyptus oil helps gorillas fight off coughs and colds as it does in humans!

At the time of my visit, Kwakane was the dominant silverback of a large gorilla group consisting of 37 apes. His massive muscular frame weighs more than 200 kilograms making him the ideal protector of his large family clan.

When they are still only a few weeks old, gorilla babies maintain continuous physical contact with their mothers using their hands and feet to cling to the long fur of the female. When I was around, the mothers often turned away to protect their offspring. But this youngster was so curious that it kept peeking at me from behind its mother's back.

Mountain gorillas are easily distinguishable from one another. In addition to their individual body shapes, they can be identified by the so-called nose print. Each gorilla has different wrinkles on its face, a feature that is as unique to each individual as the human fingerprint.

On the grounds of the former Karisoke Research Center is one of the most impressive hagenia trees of the entire Virunga region. Moss, ferns and epiphytes cover the huge tree, which spreads its branches out over the grave of the famous mountain gorilla researcher, Dian Fossey.

Until her death in 1985, Dian Fossey worked tirelessly to support the survival of the last remaining mountain gorillas. Her research formed the foundation for many protection programmes and it is thanks to her activities that there is once again a stable population of these magnificent creatures.

It is not just their behaviour that makes mountain gorillas so similar to humans. Some of their body parts are also eerily akin to ours. When this female stretched her hand towards me during a midday siesta, the gesture was so familiar, as if a human had sat down next to me.

For more than half an hour I watched this female feeding. Occasionally she would just hold a leaf to her nose and smell it, as if trying to decide whether its aroma and potential flavour met her exacting standards.

As gorillas rarely eat sweet fruit, they don't suffer from tooth decay. However, with time the tarring substances in their vegetarian diet stain both teeth and tongue.

What does this extended finger mean? A threatening gesture because I got too close to him? Unlikely. Ryango, a silverback, did not seem very impressed when he noticed me watching him from about 10 metres away. Calm and composed, he continued to groom his fur.

GELADAS

SURVIVAL IN THE HIGH MOUNTAINS

The Ethiopian Highlands are relatively barren. The landscape is mostly treeless and bleak, with dry grasslands covering the mountainous slopes. The people living here do not even raise cattle as there would not be enough food for them. And certainly the last thing one would expect to find in these high mountains is monkeys. Nevertheless, hundreds of geladas can often be found grazing here like a herd of cattle in a pasture. Their movements are almost mechanical, using both hands to grab blades of grass and place them in their mouths – up to an astounding 150 times per minute. In fact, geladas are the only monkeys that have specialized in this type of food.

PAGE 39

For years the vagaries of war in the borderlands between Ethiopia and Eritrea prevented my journey to the geladas *(Theropithecus gelada)*. This magnificent male, who was guarding his harem at the edge of a mountain grassland, was the first of these impressive primates I encountered.

PAGE 40/41/43

Nowhere in the world have I experienced tranquility as intensely as in the Simien Mountains National Park in Ethiopia. At altitudes of 4,000 metres, even the humming of a bee seemed intrusive to my ears. Viewed from the highland plateau, the ragged mountain tops rise from the valley like chiselled sculptures.

Occasionally these fascinating creatures can be seen from the winding mountain roads, but cars do not disturb the geladas. In these highlands, at altitudes of more than 3,000 metres, they require large amounts of grass and spend the better part of the day devoting all their attention to nothing but eating. It is also obvious from their behaviour that they have no need to fear humans anyway: they are neither hunted for meat or fur, nor eradicated as pests.

As there are very few trees up here, geladas probably spend more time on the ground than any other primates. As a result, they are not very good climbers, but they are quite nimble on their hands and feet. Their arms and hands are shorter than those of their tree-climbing relatives and their fingers are stubby and strong, enabling them to pull nutritious roots out of the ground even in the dry season. This does not mean they cannot climb. Indeed, geladas – who are closely related to baboons and mangabeys – scamper up incredibly steep precipices every evening to seek shelter from jackals and the Ethiopian wolf.

They are not very good at jumping, but they can pull themselves up with their sharp claws. Thus they are well adapted to life in the highlands, not least because of their thick coat of soft, thick fur that keeps them warm on cold nights at high altitudes. The males also have a long mane and bearded cheeks. The bare red patch of skin on their chests, which is especially large on male geladas and shaped like an hourglass, is unique and has given rise to the nickname "bleeding heart baboon." It is a visual sign used for communication within the species. For example, when a gelada male is agitated and wants to intimidate an opponent, he raises his upper lip and shows his enormous canine teeth. During this display his red chest becomes even brighter. On females, the intensity of the "bleeding breast" increases when they are on heat. These signals are common in monkeys that live in large troops. In female baboons, for example, a red swollen rump signals the mating period. Monkeys and apes that live in monogamous pairs or in small family groups, on the other hand, have no need for such signals.

The social structure of these highland monkeys is as unusual as their feeding habits. They typically live in harems of up to twenty animals, but these bands sometimes join together to form groups of up to 600 members, a size usually found only in large hoofed animals like antelopes or bovines. Despite their impressive size, males are not dominant in the gelada social structure. It is the females who dominate and even initiate the mating period. Typically, all of the females in a troop give birth at the same time so that their offspring can form "nursery" groups, which are more easily supervised and protected. The males then safeguard the troop using their massive teeth as a primary weapon. In fact, even leopards avoid geladas, who are quite capable of defending themselves.

Geladas feed almost exclusively on grass. In the dry season they pull the withered blades as well as the roots out of the ground to get to the more juicy bits.

PAGE 46/47
I left my tent one misty morning and came upon a troop of geladas after an hour's walk. To my surprise, I was greeted by a herd of over 100 animals grazing on a plain amid giant lobelias. These monkeys typically live in harems or single-male groups with up to 20 individuals, or sometimes the groups join to form larger troops.

The long, thick fur on these highland monkeys protects them from frosty nights and the biting winds that blow across the Ethiopian high plains.

PAGE 49
It would take my breath away whenever I watched young geladas playing on the edge of massive cliffs. I was sure these young, inexperienced adolescents were just one shove away from plummeting to their deaths. Of course, my fears were completely unfounded and they managed to romp and frolic safely despite the obvious dangers.

PAGE 50/51
As soon as young gelada males have grown up, the dominant male expels them from the harem group. The outcasts then form bachelor groups and roam the area of the harem waiting for the chance to depose their former leader.

While following a bachelor group, two males settled down next to me and started to groom each other. It didn't seem to matter that they were of the same sex. Close body contact strengthens the bonds between them and calms them down when they are agitated.

PAGE 53
The alpha male of a harem has first rights in selecting his mating partners.

Among geladas, the offspring are typically organized into "nursery groups" while their mothers graze.

I was surprised again and again to see how content these monkeys and their offspring seem to be in this barren habitat. Geladas don't have access to a large selection of food in these mountains higher than 3,000 metres. On top of that, it hardly rains from November to April.

The sun had already set when I saw this gelada male perched on a dangerous precipice – behind him is a vertical drop of 1,000 metres. Then, suddenly, a last ray of sunlight broke through the gap in the mountains and bathed this marvellous specimen in beautiful hues of gold.

Geladas spend their nights on ledges tucked into inaccessible cliffs that protect them from predators like jackals and Ethiopian wolves.

Every day I walked for miles across the craggy plateau of the Simien Mountains National Park. When the sun had disappeared below the horizon it was time to return to my tent.

With an exposure time of several hours I was able to capture the movement of the stars behind a tree. To get this shot I spent the whole night wrapped in a warm sleeping bag under a glorious sky.

CHIMPANZEES

WAR AND PEACE AMONG APES

Chimpanzees are very temperamental. They are easily annoyed and often keen for a good fight, but they are also eager peacemakers and are quick to reconcile their differences. A typical example: two female chimpanzees are sitting together grooming one another. Suddenly a male appears, jumps on the shoulders of one of the females and screaming loudly beats her for no obvious reason. Soon afterwards, he sits down next to the very same female he has just beaten and begins grooming her affectionately – and getting pampered in return as if nothing had happened!

PAGE 63
Kris was the first chimpanzee *(Pan troglodytes)* that I encountered in the wild. His imposing appearance led me to speculate immediately that he was a high-ranking member of his group. Back at the camp I was told that he had indeed just become its leader.

PAGE 64/65
The dense rainforest of the Kakombe Valley in Tanzania's Gombe National Park has a wide variety of fruit-bearing trees that offer perfect living conditions for chimpanzees.

Gombe National Park is one of the best places for observing chimpanzees in the wild. With an area of only 52 sq.km it is the smallest of Tanzania's National Parks, but accommodates more than 90 individuals of this endangered ape species, which are now accustomed to humans.

Chimpanzees are the most exhaustively researched apes, so this type of event is well documented. Jane Goodall, who has been observing chimpanzee life with her team for more than forty years in Gombe National Park in Tanzania, describes one female whom she considers a real "peacemaker." Once this female took turns grooming two males who had just had a fight. After a while the two "troublemakers" moved quite close together and eventually began grooming each other as a sign of friendship. Mutual grooming is only one of the many options for chimpanzees to make peace. They also have a gesture in their repertoire that appears very human: an open, extended hand that seems to ask for forgiveness.

Indeed, such gestures of conciliation and understanding are essential for chimpanzees precisely because they are so prone to aggression. One factor in this dynamic is that they live in highly flexible groups characterized by a steady influx and outflow of members, a so-called "fission-fusion society." An average chimpanzee troop of some forty animals does not remain together all the time. Instead, individual animals tend to roam in smaller bands or sometimes even alone.

This leads to new chance encounters that include extensive greeting ceremonies. It is customary in male chimpanzees, for example, to touch each other's testicles, all without any sexual implications. Chimpanzee troops are male-dominated networks in which each ape builds up alliances with others. The males of one troop are usually all related – brothers, half-brothers, sons or grandsons. They remain in the group that they were born into for their whole lives, whereas the females leave the group as soon as they reach sexual maturity.

The primary role of male chimpanzees is to work together in defending the group's territory against neighbouring troops. They even go on regular patrols to secure the perimeters of their domains. Typically, things will kick off when they spot neighbouring groups that are fewer in numbers! In the 1970s Jane Goodall observed how one chimpanzee troop systematically eradicated a neighbouring band. It was an ongoing battle, a "four-year war" in which the foreign chimpanzees were brutally killed and maimed.

As for food, chimpanzees eat mainly fruits, herbs, and leaves. It used to be thought that they were exclusively vegetarian, but it now appears that they sometimes have an appetite for meat. On such occasions they use twigs as tools to fish termites out of their mounds, for example, or even organize hunts in which several members of a troop chase another primate – a baboon or colobus monkey – up a tree, trap it and then kill it for food. Over the years, it has been established that chimpanzees eat an average of 11 kilograms of meat each year. In many respects, chimpanzees are very much like humans. This is not really a surprise, though, since 98 per cent of their genetic make-up is identical to ours.

Inch by inch I crawled carefully towards this chimpanzee mother and child. While I was lying on the ground waiting for the right moment to take a photo, the youngster suddenly came out from behind its mother to get a better look at its surroundings.

PAGE 70/71
Chimpanzees are tireless. In their daily search for food they trek long distances through overgrown, pathless terrain. They do stop for breaks, however, and even enjoy a relaxing stretch on the ground.

I had observed a small band of chimpanzees for more than an hour during their midday siesta. One of the youngsters suddenly decided to come closer and closer and finally leaned comfortably against a root right in front of me. It was almost too close, actually, as visitors in Gombe are supposed to keep a safe distance in order to protect the animals. These primates are so closely related to us that they can even catch diseases from human visitors.

PAGE 73
This young chimpanzee was completely focused on grooming when I came across him in the Kakombe Valley. When he finally noticed me I managed to snap just a few shots before he vanished into the dense bush.

Frodo, former leader of his troop, has become a real celebrity through Jane Goodall's research. On a hot day during the rainy season I met the elderly, greying chimpanzee sitting in the dense undergrowth. Soon afterwards, he lay down for his siesta just 10 metres away from me.

Chimpanzees are the closest relatives of humans in the animal kingdom: 98.5 per cent of their genome is identical to that of humans. When dealing with other members of their species they can be as aggressive as we are. Strategically organized, violent disputes – downright wars even – between different troops have been observed consistently over the years.

PAGE 77
On several occasions I had noticed a tree trunk spanning a dry river bed and assumed that the apes would use it as a bridge. My guess was right. One day Kris led his whole group over the trunk to the other bank. To my great delight, he stopped for a few seconds to take a closer look at the forest on the opposite side of he bridge.

Every day I had to track down the chimpanzees from "my" group in the Kakombe Valley. Once I had finally found them it was very exhausting trying to keep up with them on steep slopes in dense undergrowth. It was only when they stopped to rest that I was able to get down to the business of taking photographs.

Young chimpanzees have faces with very fair skin. With age the skin grows darker and even almost black in some individuals.

Male chimpanzees repeatedly show pronounced display behaviour to impress their peers and achieve a higher rank in the group. During these shows, they try to make as much of a racket as possible, snapping branches of rotten wood and pulling and rattling on lianas.

One afternoon I observed a female leaning against a tree. She seemed to be lost in thought and in deep contemplation before finally returning to the group and continuing to look for food. It is always a very special experience to watch wild chimpanzees at close range. I never had the feeling of being an unwelcome guest.

At a termite mound I witnessed how chimpanzees use tools: some of them stripped the bark off twigs and then used them to fish termites out of the mound. With incredible skill they teased out the delicious tit-bits one by one and managed to put together a good protein-rich meal. They learn this method as adolescents, using their tools with dexterity and patience.

Depending on their habitat, chimpanzees enjoy up to 200 different plant species as food and have to be able to recognize them all in order to distinguish them from the inedible ones. A particular favourite in Gombe is the fruit of the rubber vine *(Saba florida)*, called "mabungo" in Swahili. It has been proven that the apes use some plant species as proper medicine for pain or nausea. They are not absolute vegetarians, however, occasionally hunting monkeys, bushbucks and other mammals.

PAGE 86
Chimpanzees spend about half of their time on the ground. During the other half they climb trees, mainly to pick fruit. This young chimpanzee sat on the trunk of a fallen tree and watched me cross a river.

Giant rainforest trees grow in many places in Gombe. The enormous buttress roots of these glorious specimens never cease to impress me.

The Kakombe Waterfall is one of the landmarks of Gombe National Park. It tumbles over a cliff in the valley of the same name.

Chimpanzee mothers protect their young very vigilantly. This baby is seeking refuge in the arms of its mother while Frodo, the former leader of the group, makes a racket in the canopy of an old tree.

Chimpanzees are extremely observant. Only rarely were they surprised by my arrival. They usually spotted me long before I saw them.

One rainy afternoon I noticed a female chimpanzee with two youngsters in their sleeping nest. Not wanting to miss the moment, I crawled up a muddy hill where I found a gap in the dense canopy and was able to capture this intimate family scene.

Asia

JAPANESE MACAQUES

HANUMAN LANGURS

ORANG-UTANS

ORANG-UTANS

INVENTORS AND THINKERS

Observing the great apes of Asia in the wild is one of the primatologists' most diffi-cult tasks. In fact, these "forest people" – in Malay "orang" means person and "hutan" means forest – spend most of their lives 30 metres above ground in the towering canopy. Indonesians even believe that the main reason that the "forest people" do not talk is to avoid being drafted into work. When a human gets too close for comfort, they drop branches or other objects on their unwanted guests. This behaviour makes it all the more difficult to closely observe these fascinating creatures.

PAGE 95

During my visit to Borneo, Kusasi was the dominant male orang-utan *(Pongo pygmaeus)* in the area around the Camp Leakey research station. But even then there was a takeover on the horizon. Kusasi's best days were over, and soon a younger male would take his position.

Orang-utans, which can weigh up to 90 kilograms, are the heaviest animals to spend so much of their time in the treetops. Only very rarely do these red apes venture down to the ground. When they want to travel across a gap between trees, they prefer to swing on the tree's branches until they are able to grab a small twig of the next tree with their out-stretched arm. Then they pull the twig towards them until they reach a branch that is strong enough to support their weight and climb over to it slowly and carefully. They hardly ever risk great leaps across gaps in the canopy like the leaner gibbons do. Despite their diligence, however, the "forest people" still seem to make the occasional blunder. We know of these sporadic bouts of clumsiness from healed bone fractures in the skeletons of orang-utans in museum collections.

PAGE 96/97

My favourite time to visit the tropical primeval forests is the rainy season, when everything is saturated with water, the leaves on the trees are luscious and glistening, and rain or mist transforms the forest into a mystical scene. It seems to me the truest version of a rainforest.

Orang-utans give birth after 230 to 260 days of pregnancy and from the first day the bond between mother and child is incredibly close. Not until the youngsters are three or four years old will they be fully weaned.

Socially, orang-utans are considered complete loners. Only the young like to play with their mates while adults prefer to roam around on their own. In par-ticular, adult males live solitary lives, spending much of their time marking territory against rivals with thunderous calls. The impressive cheek pads combined with a unique throat pouch help to amplify these signals. Within each male's territory there

are typically several females who roam in smaller areas with their offspring looking for food, mostly fruits and other vegetarian delights. Occasionally they will also indulge in an egg or a few bugs.

For a long time, orang-utans were thought of as obstinate, dull and introverted, not like their lively and "intelligent" relatives, the chimps. But their image has changed over the years, particularly through observations made in zoos where we have learned that orang-utans possess some exceptional technical skills. Within a matter of minutes each evening, for example, they will build a new nest from twigs and branches to sleep in. They even find solutions to rather intricate problems. Orang-utans have been known to disassemble locks on their cages with great patience and dexterity. One female even used a piece of wire to make a proper lock pick, then opened her cage and investigated the ape house. Chimpanzees would be far too frantic and impatient for such delicate technical challenges.

Only recently have we begun to discover this technical intelligence in the orang-utan's natural environment. Orang-utans in the wild have been observed using leaves as gloves to open prickly fruits or to protect themselves against sun and rain in their nests. They also make tools – a behaviour previously only observed in chimpanzees – such as small sticks to pick food out of cracks, or twigs to swat flies.

Orang-utans, the inventors and thinkers among apes, may well have more surprises for us in the future. There have been recent reports of populations of the "forest people "who lead more social and less solitary lives.

Orang-utans are skilful climbers even as babies, and they start to move independently in the canopy at an early age. However, they prefer to caper about near their mothers to test their strength.

PAGE 102/103
This orang-utan female climbed from tree to tree in search of food. Eventually she found a termite nest, broke it off the branch and delightedly started sucking the little insects out of the pod.

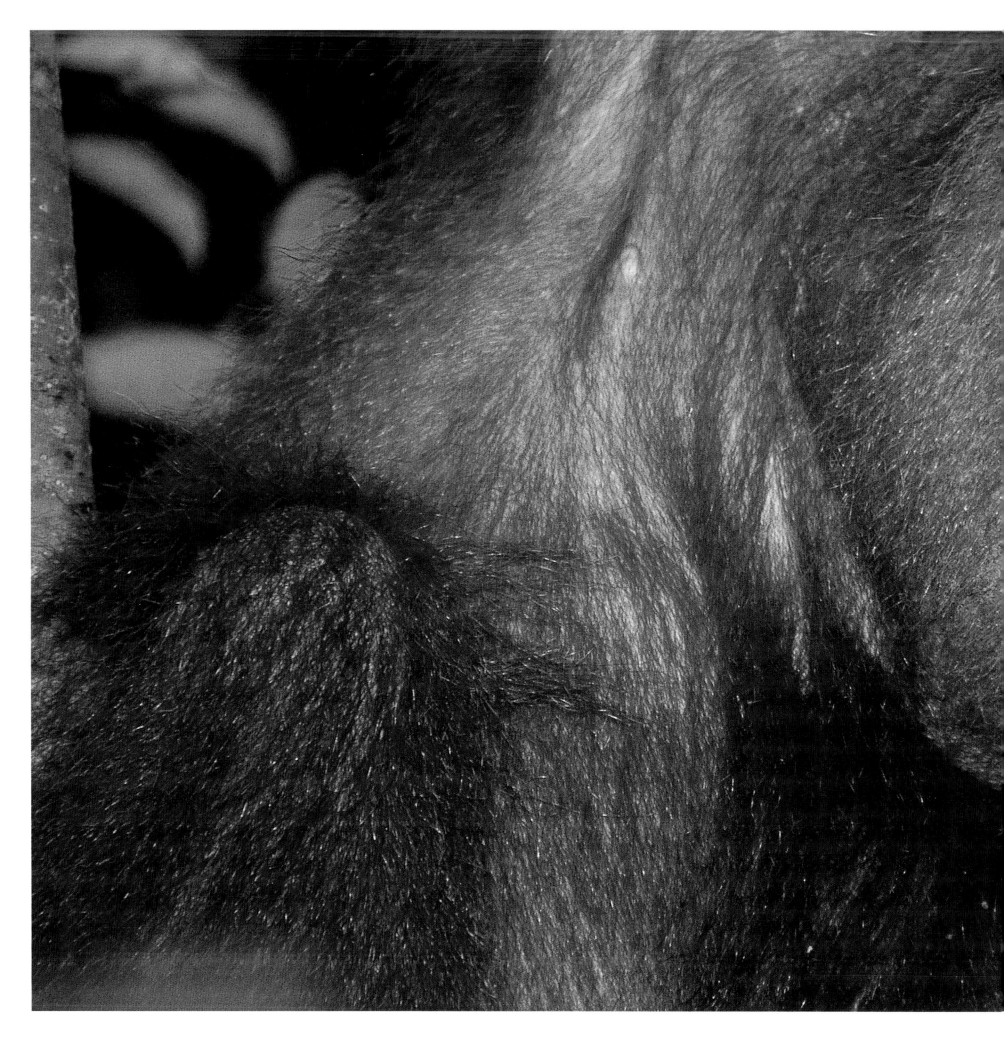

With their extremely long arms – the "wingspan" of a male orang-utan can reach two and a half metres – these apes are able to cross large gaps in the canopy by climbing from one tree to the next.

A faint rustling indicated the presence of an orang-utan female with her baby. She must have spotted me much earlier, but was obviously undisturbed by my presence.

PAGE 106/107
Orang-utans are extremely skilful with their hands. Like chimpanzees they have been observed using tools on many occasions.

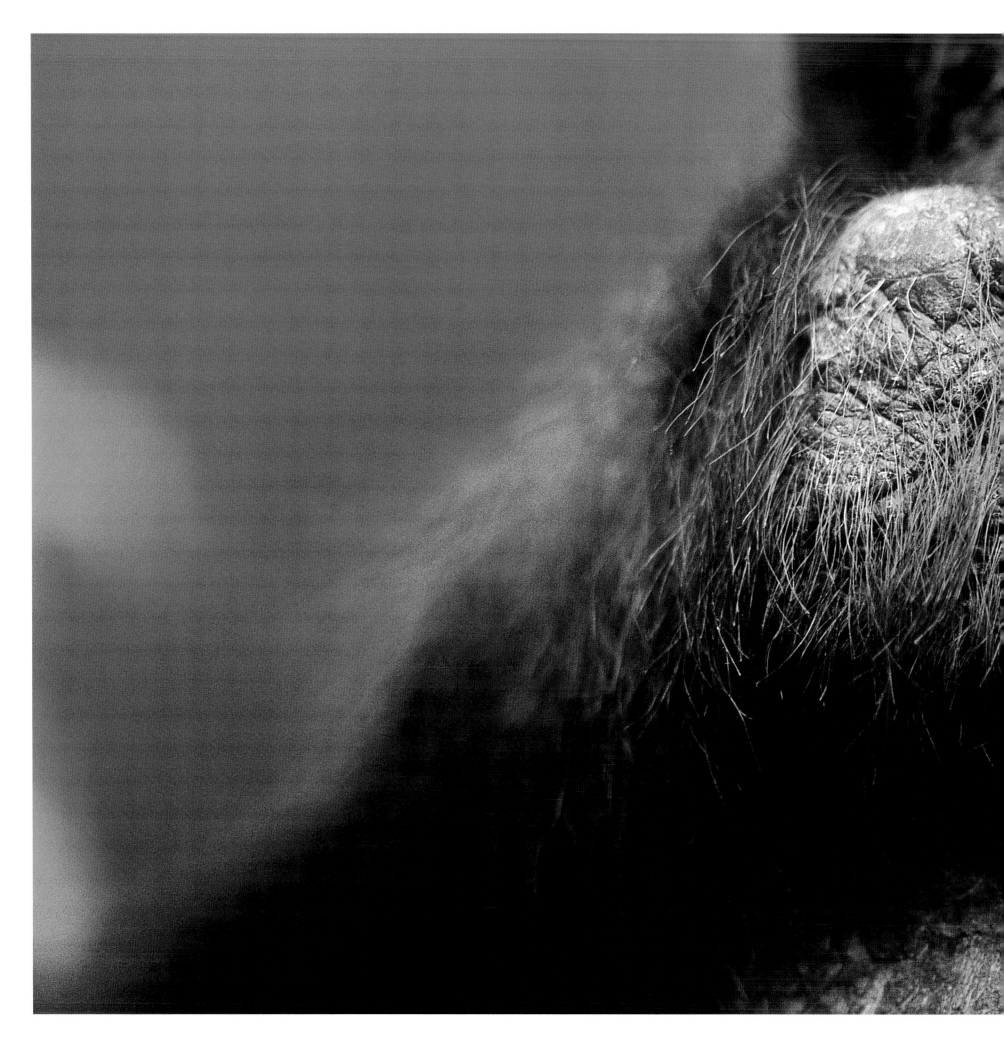

I had hoped for a long time to take a photo of an orang-utan with outstretched arms, backlit to create an outline of bright light. The opportunity presented itself just once: the day before I left Borneo.

The Tanjung Puting National Park, with an area of more than 3,000 sq.km in the south of Borneo, is one of the last reserves for orang-utans in the wild. But even here the last sizeable, intact forests are threatened by illegal logging.

PAGE 110/111
Orang-utan males weigh up to 100 kilograms and are twice as heavy as the females. The most apparent difference between the sexes is the shape of the face. When they get older, males develop formidable cheek pads consisting of connective tissue.

Blackwater rivers flow through the thick jungles of Tanjung Puting National Park. I spent my nights on a small boat on the river and went on land only to take photographs.

I was able to catch this orang-utan building a nest to sleep in. By cleverly twisting and weaving twigs together, these apes are able to build a comfortable shelter for the night within a matter of minutes. Usually they construct a new one every evening.

JAPANESE MACAQUES

WINTER IS THE HOT SPRINGS' SEASON

Asia

Everything was different in the old days. Just a few decades ago Japanese macaques, or snow monkeys, migrated every winter from the summits of the Japanese Alps down into the lower lying forests. But then the forests where the monkeys used to spend the cold season were logged and the trees made way for the ski slopes of the Nagano Winter Olympics. It must have been around this time that the macaques discovered the joys of warm water.

PAGE 115
I did not have to search for long in the snowy forests of Japan's Jigokudani Yaen-Koen ("Hell Valley Monkey Park") to find the famous Japanese macaques *(Macaca fuscata)*. Indeed, I shall never forget my first glimpse of these extraordinary monkeys, with their thick grey fur and bright red faces.

PAGE 116/117
In winter, the craggy slopes of Hell Valley in the Japanese Alps are covered in deep snow and temperatures fall to minus 20°C (-4°F), an unusual habitat for monkeys. Fortunately, natural hot springs make the climate bearable for these unique macaques.

Although the snow monkeys are used to humans, it still took several days before I could get a close-up of a macaque mother with her young one.

How it started, nobody knows for sure. Legend has it that a sailor once enjoyed bathing in the hot springs in Jigokudani ("Hell Valley"), part of the Joshinetsu Plateau National Park, and the macaques simply "aped" his behaviour. Soon, more and more of the local snow monkeys began visiting the 40°C (104°F) springs to stay warm in their freezing, snowy surroundings. The snow monkeys then became a tourist attraction, and people flocked to the spa to observe the monkeys' "bathing culture" – and, of course, to enjoy the hot springs themselves. Nowadays in the so-called Jigokudani Yaen-Koen ("Hell Valley Monkey Park"), the monkeys have been given their own pool, for reasons of hygiene, and can be observed more easily as they relax in the comfortable thermal baths.

For researchers of animal behaviour, Japanese macaques are a prime example of the ability of primates to adapt, and it is not only in Hell Valley that they have learned to master relatively abrupt changes in their natural environment. In other parts of Japan they also established their own "culture" – a term that many prefer to reserve for humans. In fact, snow monkeys have developed many forms of human-like behaviour. They initially became famous after Japanese scientists began observing them in the 1950s on the island of Koshima. Since then, researchers have examined the social life of

macaques for several decades, recording both changes in behaviour and the emergence of new "fashions." To accustom the monkeys to the presence of humans, the scientists fed the monkeys wheat at the beach. However, picking the grains out of the sand proved a laborious task, so one day a particularly bright young female macaque had the idea of washing the sand off in a nearby creek. Taking a handful of grain, she threw it into the water – with amazing results. She was able to filter the food from the surface without any unpleasant debris. Other members of the group soon mimicked her idea. But that was only the beginning. Another monkey "washed" sweet potatoes given to him by scientists in the ocean, not in the creek. This not only cleaned the potatoes of sand, but also gave them a salty flavour. The monkey had discovered the salt potato! Again, the other monkeys in the group soon imitated this new, improved dish.

Initially this behaviour spread from younger animals to older ones, from youngsters to mothers. In monkeys, as in humans, the youngest are the most curious and adaptable individuals. The older males, who were most concerned with rank in the troop, naturally took longest to acquire the new behaviour but soon the whole group had learned to wash food. A few years later, every newborn learned from its mother to wash potatoes in the ocean as part of the normal ritual, as if this had always been the way. The "invention" was passed down to the next generation and a local "tradition" had begun. These are some of the things that make it possible for Japanese macaques to live farther north than any other monkeys. But other species also live in cold mountain ranges that initially seem inhospitable: the Assam macaques in the Himalayas or the Barbary macaques in the High Atlas Mountains of North Africa. Macaques are particularly inventive and adaptive "creatures of culture."

With great skill this adolescent monkey was able to pull a stick out of the snow and proceed to munch on the bark. In the freezing cold, these animals can't be fussy and are forced to eat whatever they can get their hands on.

PAGE 122/123
Apparently, it was only about fifty years ago that the first snow monkey took a dip in the 43°C hot springs in Hell Valley. Since then a real bathing culture has evolved, with young and old macaques gathering in the warm waters to relax and groom each other.

The rays of the low winter sun do not reach all the way down to the floor of Hell Valley. In these freezing temperatures this young monkey seeks the warmth of his mother's furry embrace.

Although a dense fog reduced visibility in the valley to almost nil, the mystical ambience was an inspiration. I wouldn't really call myself a "fair weather photographer" – I prefer cloudy, misty days with soft light.

Japanese macaques spend their nights in the trees that grow around the slopes of the valley. Their sharp nails allow them to climb vertical tree trunks without difficulty.

PAGE 127/128/129
For the monkeys in the Jigokudani Yaen-Koen, or Hell Valley Monkey Park, a separate pool has been built in one of the hot springs. The animals would probably survive the hard winter without this support, but they appear to enjoy the relaxing warm water.

This elderly female macaque appeared completely
drenched and miserable on leaving the water, but
in just five minutes her fur was completely dry . I
got the impression that the older the monkeys,
the more time they spent in the hot springs.

PAGE 131
A macaque baby clings to its mother's fur
during their search for food in the deep snow.

With their thick fur, snow monkeys are well adapted to the extreme winter conditions in Hell Valley. They even manage to survive snow-storms unharmed. My camera equipment, on the other hand, suffered: the batteries in particular discharged very much faster in such low temperatures.

When I got to the snow monkeys' pool at dawn, the early risers were already enjoying the warm waters. On particularly frosty days they extended their bathing times and left the spring only to get food.

PAGE 135
The hot spring in Hell Valley is used by some 200 monkeys. Nevertheless, after only a few days I was able to recognize some of the more frequent guests individually.

HANUMAN LANGURS

"HOLY" IN NAME ONLY

Monkeys are particularly easy to observe in India. In this densely populated country, they even live among humans in the cities, and not just in the "green" parklands of the temple precincts. It is not at all uncommon to find them roaming the streets of megacities like Delhi or Mumbai. In fact, they are not only tolerated but actually often cared for by the local population – they are regarded as holy animals in Hinduism. The Hanuman langurs (also called grey or common langurs) are in fact named after the monkey god Hanuman. Devout Hindus even feed them, which often results in some pretty cheeky and self-confident behaviour. They frequently raid farmers' fields or pilfer fruit from the market, but this is accepted by the locals. However, in their original habitat, the semi-arid Thar Desert in the state of Rajasthan, food is scarce and the langurs have specialized in eating leaves, which are not very rich in nutrients. To be able to utilize this meagre diet effectively they have developed a stomach with different chambers similar to that of ruminants, and bacteria in the stomach aid digestion.

PAGE 139

Newborn Hanuman langurs *(Semnopithecus entellus)* have black and brown fur. This baby clung to its mother's pelt continuously. It usually takes a few weeks before the young start to investigate the surrounding areas on their own.

PAGE 140/141/143

The Hanuman langurs – sacred monkeys of India – are common all over the subcontinent and well adapted to different habitats. In the Indian state of Rajasthan, I observed them in the temple ruins of Jodhpur.

Socially, troops of Hanuman langurs are organized in strict hierarchies. Typically one "monarch" is the leader, protecting the females and youngsters from enemies and other langur males. Preferably he has his fur groomed by the higher-ranking female members of the troop, but the females are also considerate of one another. They take joint care of their young, which have darker fur in their first weeks, in proper "nurseries." Despite appearing peaceful at first glance, however, the social life of Hanuman langurs can be chaotic. Outside the family groups there are always young single males roaming about who haven't been able to form harems – and therefore have no chance to breed. Again and again these bachelors will try – either alone or in small packs – to challenge the leader of a harem group and brutal fights can ensue. With their sharp teeth these

monkeys can inflict gaping, bloody wounds. Long-term studies in Rajasthan have shown that the average "term of office" for a harem leader is only 26 months. He is usually then deposed in a violent coup and expelled. As soon as the takeover is complete, the alliance of the adolescent bachelors then breaks down, as only one of them can become the new leader of the harem group. The bloody tussle therefore does not end with the simple overthrow. In fact, this is where the real drama begins. The new leader then hunts down newborn and unweaned youngsters and kills all infants that were sired by his predecessor. Their mothers try desperately to defend their offspring, often supported by other females, but sooner or later the new "monarch" succeeds in killing most of the young.

Such infanticide can be observed in baboons and chimpanzees too, but it is not limited to primates. Lions practise it as well. The explanation for this gruesome behaviour is that the new leader has only a limited time to produce his own offspring before being deposed himself. He must therefore use the time of his "reign" as efficiently as possible – the earlier the females are receptive again, the more successful he will be in passing on his genes. The goal is not the survival of the species, but the spreading of his own genes. The mothers initially mourn their dead babies, but soon their hormones switch from nursing back to reproduction. And, because it is also in the interest of the female to procreate again as quuickly as possible, they soon – often just a month after the massacre – mate again with the new leader, who will later defend his offspring by all necessary means. If they are lucky, the next power struggle will occur after the new generation has grown old enough to be spared from the killing. The Hanuman langurs are therefore by no means "holy" in their behaviour. On the contrary, they behave with as much self-interest as any other living being on earth.

It was the vast expanse and magical light of the Thar Desert that made my first trip to India such a unique experience. For six weeks I tracked a group of Hanuman langurs from dawn till dusk.

PAGE 146/147
Luckily I was able to follow a troop that had become accustomed by an Indian scientist to the presence of humans. After only a few days I was able to linger among them at a distance of just a few metres.

These two young monkeys watched me curiously while I was setting up my camera. When I had finished, they stayed for a few seconds, just long enough for me to take this portrait.

Langur mothers help each other in raising their young. They regularly look after the children of other females so they all have some spare time to search for food.

The little monkeys have a blissful childhood protected by their mothers and the whole group – unless the leader of the harem changes.

One morning, a zebu cow had entered the territory of the monkey troop. As it attempted to raid the langurs' food, the leader of the group attacked it and chased it away.

Their long arms and legs make the Hanuman langurs very fast runners. **The raised tail helps them keep their balance.**

During my second visit to the langurs of the Thar Desert I happened to run straight into a confrontation between the leader of a harem and a pack of bachelors. I was right on the frontline when the fight erupted and the animals began gunning for each other. My reflex was to shield myself with the tripod. At the end of the fight, the old leader had succeeded in defending his position in the harem, but had suffered some nasty wounds.

PAGE 154/155
Mutual grooming has little to do with "louse picking." Often the monkeys pick only dandruff or dirt from each other's fur.

Langurs prefer to spend the night on a steep cliff where they are safe from stray dogs. Usually I left the group at dusk, once the monkeys had settled down on the narrow ledges for the evening, and then returned the next morning before the first rays of sunlight were upon them.

PAGE 157
Although the langurs are accustomed to the presence of humans, it was a few days before they allowed me to photograph intimate situations such as breastfeeding at close range.

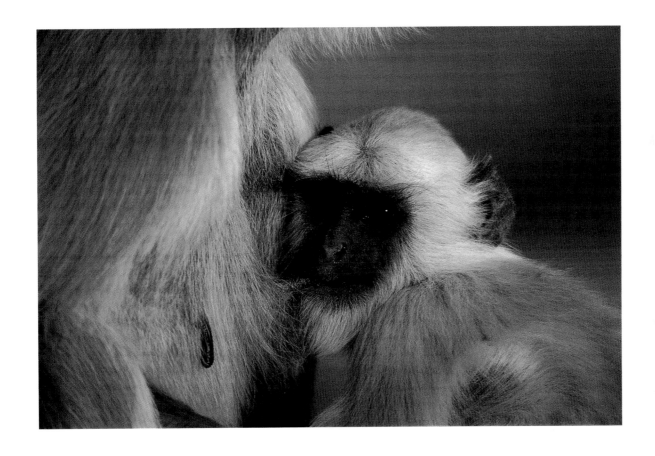

Usually a female Hanuman langur gives birth every two years. Twins are extremely rare.

These "sacred" monkeys live in troops of ten to forty individuals. Depending on the size of the group and the lie of the land, their territory can range up to 20 sq.km.

PAGE 160
After a cold night in the desert the langurs like to warm up in the morning sun. I found this group huddled on a rock lit by a ray of light that shone through a gap in the cliff. When they noticed me, they all looked into my camera simultaneously for a few seconds.

In the last light of the evening sun this adolescent perches on the edge of his sleeping rock, as if enjoying the last rays of sun before climbing to his spot on the cliff for the night.

SPIDER MONKEYS

RED UAKARIS

South America

SPIDER MONKEYS

164

RED UAKARIS

180

SPIDER MONKEYS

AERIAL ACROBATS

Observing spider monkeys in the wild is not always easy, but not because they are rare. In fact, they are quite common in the forests and jungles of the New World. The problem for an observer is that they are very rarely anywhere but high up in the towering rainforest canopy some 30 to 50 metres above the ground. In their aerial element, you glimpse them only fleetingly as they "fly" from treetop to treetop with elegant leaps and sweeping lunges of up to 10 metres. Their speed and agility make it almost impossible to follow their movements from the ground. While you are tackling the thicket with your machete, the spider monkeys dangle and swing like circus acrobats in the canopy, far outpacing any progress you may be making. Since the tops of the tallest trees are often connected by liana vines, the monkeys move virtually unhindered through the dense vegetation.

PAGE 165

A long prehensile tail provides spider monkeys with a virtual "fifth limb," which they use for a variety of things. When I spotted this young Geoffroy's spider monkey *(Ateles geoffroy*, also called black-handed spider monkey) in the thick forest canopy, it had taken a seat on its own tail.

The tropical dry forests of Santa Rosa National Park, covering an area of 50 sq.km in northern Costa Rica, offer a wealth of animal life and food – an ideal habitat for the many types of monkey living there.

Spider monkeys are perfectly adapted for life on high. Although their body length can reach nearly a metre, they are exceptionally lean, rarely weighing more than eight kilograms. And with disproportionately long arms and legs they are easily able to grab distant branches, twigs or vines. The fingers on their hook-shaped hands, in fact, are permanently bent, a special adaptation to their arboreal lifestyle that inherently prevents them from losing their grip when swinging through the trees. As a result of this development, however, their thumbs are dramatically reduced in size and not opposable, making it difficult for them to grasp objects with any real dexterity. Indeed, an opposable thumb would prove to be a disadvantage to their mobility as it could be easily sprained or fractured. Zoologists regarded this detached thumb as so characteristic that it inspired the scientific genus given to these monkeys: ateles, meaning "thumbless." To compensate for their detached thumb, spider monkeys possess a sort of fifth "limb" – their long prehensile tails.

Only a few other closely related species of New World monkeys have evolved such a defined prehensile tail, namely the woolly monkeys and the muriqui or woolly spider monkeys. In Darwinian terms, the spider monkey's tail is a perfect adaptation. It is longer than the arms and legs, which considerably extends their reach, and strong enough to support the full body weight of these acrobatic climbers. They have a special grip pad on the hairless inner side of the tip to give them a better hold on branches and vines, and it is even occasionally used as a precision instrument, ultimately compensating for some of the finer motor functions that are impossible with their unopposable thumb. Spider monkeys in captivity, for example, have been observed using their tails to grab very small objects such as peanuts through a fence and bringing them to their mouths.

With this versatile "tool," spider monkeys are made for life in the imposing canopy. When they are not "flying" through the trees they are rather careful climbers, when foraging, for instance, and generally use three or four limbs to maintain a firm hold. Their main diet of fruit is found high up in the trees along with other delights such as new leaves, buds and flowers. But they are not strict vegetarians. Sometimes insects and their larva form part of their culinary repertoire.

Midday was the only time the spider monkeys took a short siesta; for the rest of the day they moved swiftly and skilfully through the rainforest canopy. Only with the help of experienced local scientists was I able to track them effectively .

In their natural habitat these monkeys hardly ever leave the trees. In fact, their movements are rather clumsy on the ground where the prehensile tail is of no use to them. Although able to "soar" 10 metres in the canopy, they are hardly able to jump over a ditch 2 metres wide on the ground. Swimming is also not their strong suit. As a result, the various major rivers of Central and South America have formed effective frontiers around which several unique species and subspecies of spider monkeys have evolved – the thumbless specialists of the treetops.

Spider monkeys use their long tails for balance and to get a good grip on the branches.

Downpours were quite frequent during my stay in Santa Rosa National Park in Costa Rica, but the bad weather did not stop the monkeys from searching for food.

173

Strangler figs, which can actually kill their host tree, are common in many parts of Santa Rosa National Park.

A waterproof pack to keep my camera dry was an essential part of my equipment. I had to wait an hour for the rain to stop before photographing these glistening golden roots.

The scientists and I left camp before dawn on a chilly day when we found a group of spider monkeys huddled together to keep warm.

Spider monkeys eat mostly ripe fruit, but also seeds and leaves. Occasionally they add insects or birds' eggs to their menu.

Photo opportunities as good as this one were a rarity. Spider monkeys typically stay high up in the trees where they are hidden by dense vegetation.

RED UAKARIS

WHERE "UGLY" MEANS HEALTHY

The first time you see a red uakari is unforgettable: a bald monkey with a bright crimson face and thick bulges on its forehead, a stocky body with a bushy stump for a tail that seems far too short to be of any use, and an infinitely sad expression. The Brazilians call the red uakari "macaco inglês" – or "English monkey" – because it looks rather like the eccentric, gin-drinking rubber barons and early European explorers who burned their fair skin in the hot South American sun. However that may be, red uakaris do not exactly make an endearing first impression. To the untrained eye they actually look old, sick and rather ridiculous.

But appearances can be deceiving. These monkeys, which are roughly the size of large cats, are not at all sickly or weak, but in robust health. Their fur is bright orange, which makes them the most colourful monkeys in all of South America. Until recently, however, only very little was known about the lifestyle of these "baldheads." The reason for the mystery was that red uakaris live in a very remote basin of the Rio Yavarí in the border region between Peru and Brazil, and it is only in the last few years that researchers have begun studying them seriously.

Red uakaris roam the forests in troops of up to fifty animals, each troop consisting of subgroups of one male each with several females. They live mostly high up in the trees at heights of 30 to 50 metres. During their search for food they usually keep a distance of a few metres from each other. On occasion, large gatherings of more than 200 monkeys occur, particularly in places where food is plentiful. Uakaris are equipped with exceptionally strong jaws that are perfect

PAGE 181

After two days and more than 10 kilometres of exhausting treks through the forest, I finally saw my first red uakari *(Cacajao calvus)*. I had long hoped for this moment and cherished the chance to observe these extremely rare and beautiful animals in the wild.

PAGE 182/183

Palm swamps are the preferred habitat of red uakaris.

The Rio Yavarí meanders through the pristine rainforest of the Amazon basin. From Iquitos it takes one hour by seaplane or four days by boat to reach the habitat of the uakaris.

"nutcrackers," and with their robust teeth they can crack even the hardest of shells. In the palm swamps of the Rio Yavarí, however, they mainly eat the reddish fruit of Moriche palms, whose flesh is easily separated from the pits.

Curious minds will want to know why the red uakaris are red – and not just in the face. According to Richard Bodmer, who has been studying these unique monkeys of the Rio Yavarí basin for several years, one reason may be that they are scarcely visible when they hang upside down from the Moriche palms between the abundant bunches of fruit. This protects them from their most prominent predator, the harpy eagle, which specializes in preying on monkeys in treetops. The colourful fur is therefore simply a form of camouflage.

As far as their seemingly unhealthy facial colour is concerned, there appears to be a different explanation: uakari fur is coloured by pigments, but their red face is simply blood glowing through the monkey's skin. It is this that produces its truly "blood-red" complexion. When uakaris are sick, their bright red complexion dulls, and when they are dead they turn extremely pale. A vibrant bald head with bright crimson colouring therefore gives a clear signal to peers: "I'm healthy."

The most prominent feature of red uakaris is their naked heads. A crimson red face is a sign of good health.

When choosing mates this facial colour plays a particularly significant role. The brighter the face, the healthier the monkey. For females, naturally, it is especially important to find healthy, fit males to sire their offspring. For male uakaris their heads become a sort of additional "advertising" surface. The bulges on the forehead serve to create even more space to boast of their good health and vitality. Beauty is truly in the eye of the beholder!

The fruit of the Moriche palm *(Mauritia flexuosa)* is the staple food of red uakaris. In one of these palms I spotted a female with her youngster and took the first photograph ever of a wild uakari with her offspring.

Surprised by our visit this uakari shows its canine teeth. These rare monkeys have only a small habitat and have been heavily hunted, the main reason so few humans have had the opportunity to see them in the wild.

Like most New World monkeys, the uakaris are diurnal animals that spend nearly all of their time in the tops of massive jungle trees. They are skilled climbers and travel across gaps in the canopy with enormous leaps and bounds.

PAGE 192/193
Prominent bulges on the forehead show that
this uakari is an older male.

PAGE 194
Although uakaris roam the forest in large groups,
they usually keep at least a few metres' distance
from one another.

I spotted this not yet fully grown male after it
had climbed a dead tree and began rocking the
entire trunk, a typical territorial display.

Red uakaris place great demands on their
habitat. In large groups they inhabit an area
of up to 150 sq.km.

Even hard-shelled fruit is no problem
for the uakaris' long canine teeth.

PAGE 198/199

In young males the characteristic bulges on the forehead are not yet fully developed.

PAGE 200

Only when they grow older do small knobs begin to develop on the forehead giving them a more masculine look.

To survive in the forest canopy these monkeys have to be acrobatic. Uakaris often hang upside down in the trees to reach their beloved Moriche palm fruit.

PAGE 202/203

The Lago Preto Conservation Concession was established in one of the most species-rich areas of the world, along the Rio Yavari in Peru. Red uakaris in particular benefit from the protected area and can now be studied more thoroughly.

OTHER PRIMATES

A DIVERSE LOT

There are more than 280 documented species of primates in the world, from the 30-gram mouse lemur to the 270-kilogram male mountain gorilla. All of them belong to the biological order primates, a name that originally referred to their "top" ranking in the animal kingdom. It is a diverse lot that includes three groups: prosimians, New World monkeys and Old World monkeys. "Prosimians" got their slightly odd name from early scientists who, from a human perspective, saw them as less evolved than "proper" monkeys and apes – humans, of course, also belonging to primates.

From an evolutionary viewpoint, prosimians are actually quite a successful group. Many of them are solitary nocturnal insectivores. The African galagos, also called bushbabies because of their cute appearance, and the lorises and tarsiers of Asia, for example, are all typical prosimians. It may be that their predominantly nocturnal lifestyle developed as a way of avoiding competition with their "superior" diurnal primate relatives. Only Madagascar, which has no simian primates, plays host to a diverse group of diurnal prosimians. Some of the many species of lemurs also live in social groups like the beautiful ring-tailed lemurs (kattas), or the ruffed lemurs (varis) with their fox-like faces.

New World monkeys include such species as spider monkeys, tiny marmosets, tamarins and uakaris and are considered "true" monkeys. Because of their round noses and broad nasal septum they have been given the scientific name platyrrhini ("flat-nosed"). The primates of the Old World, on the other hand, have narrow nostrils and a thin septum. These "narrow-nosed" (catarrhini) creatures include guenons, langurs, macaques, baboons, apes and humans. Compared to other animals, primates possess several characteristic features. Ancestral primates were arboreal, and for their life in the forest they had to be able

PAGE 205
The small-toothed sportive lemur *(Lepilemur microdon)* of Madagascar doesn't quite look like a typical primate. When it heard me, it popped its head curiously out of its burrow, but I was only able take a few photos before the nocturnal prosimian disappeared again to safety.

PAGE 206/207
Ring-tailed lemurs, or kattas *(Lemur catta)*, are probably the most famous of the Madagascan lemurs. These social, cat-size prosimians live in the southern part of this large island.

Gombe National Park in Tanzania is also home to several troops of Anubis baboons *(Papio anubis)*. They search the shores of Lake Tanganyika systematically for seeds that are washed ashore, and crack them with their massive jaws for food.

to climb, jump and grasp branches safely without losing their grip. They therefore evolved "pentadactyl" ("five-digit") limbs in which the five fingers can be controlled independently. With these prehensile hands and feet they were able to conquer a habitat that is inaccessible to animals with hooves, for example. Equipped with these tools, primates were then able to investigate objects in detail and even "manipulate" them – a word of Latin origin that literally means "treat with the hands." Evolutionarily speaking, the dexterous opposable thumb has enabled apes (and humans) to perfect the art of using their hands.

Another important feature of primates is forward-facing eyes. Most mammals have eyes on the sides of their heads. Over the course of their evolution, primate eyes moved forward on their heads. The fields of view from both eyes then overlapped and eventually enabled three-dimensional vision. This binocular vision (or stereopsis) enables primates to estimate distances better, an enormous advantage in habitats with trees and other obstacles. Furthermore, primates are the only mammals that can see a wide spectrum of colour, making it much easier to identify different fruit and blossoms. The vibrant faces of mandrills, the crimson heads of uakaris, and the colourful genitals of guenons also indicate that colour is essential to the social displays of primates. To handle all of these capacities, primates ultimately evolved an increasingly large and complex brain.

These features eventually helped primates to populate very different habitats: the rainforests of South America, Asia and Africa, the mountain forests of East Africa, the dry forests of Central America, the Indian jungle, and the cold forests of Japan and the Atlas Mountains. Various species have even pulled out of the forest completely. Some, like the baboons and the patas monkeys of Africa, live in the savannah. Others, like the rhesus monkeys of India live in big cities. Primate diets are of a similarly diverse nature. Most are traditional "raw vegans" who consume fruits, buds and delicate leaves. The tiny marmosets of South America, for example, actually scratch through the bark with their specially adapted teeth – like a rubber tree tap – and lick the sweet sap from the incisions.

Other primates, like the colobus monkeys of Africa or the langurs of Asia, have adapted to leafy sustenance. They have even developed a stomach with different chambers, similar to that of ruminants, in which special bacteria help to extract the most nutrients possible from the meagre diet. The nocturnal galagos and tarsiers feed mostly on insects. Guenons, macaques and capuchin monkeys supplement their vegetarian diet with reptiles, birds' eggs, and even young birds. Baboons and chimpanzees dine regularly on animals such as young ungulates or other monkeys, which they deliberately hunt in groups.

Generally speaking, most primates are social animals. One exception is the solitary adult male orang-utan who typically roams the forest canopy on his own. By contrast, some species like the gibbons live in long-term monogamous relationships, although a bit of infidelity appears to be acceptable. Marmosets and tamarins are also mostly monogamous and raise their offspring together, often with the help of older siblings until they start their own families. In addition to these small family groups there are also primates that live in larger communities with distinctive hierarchies. In harem groups among Hamadryas baboons or Hanuman langurs, for example, one male leader gathers a number of females around him.

Previously unknown species of monkeys are still being discovered to this day, particularly in remote areas of the Amazon rainforest. In fact, the complete diversity of primates remains unknown.

Anubis baboon mothers care for their offspring with great devotion, rarely letting them out of sight.

The mandrill (*Mandrillus sphinx*) is one of the most colourful mammals in the world. Its face is particularly vibrant. The highest-ranking animal in the group tends to be the one with the most dynamic colours. Mandrills are closely related to baboons and live in the rainforests of West Africa.

Barbary macaques *(Macaca sylvanus)* are the only macaques living in Africa rather than Asia. The High Atlas Mountains of Morocco and Algeria are their home, but as the cedar and oak forests there are destroyed by logging activities this species is becoming increasingly threatened.

In the Gunung Leuser National Park in Sumatra I encountered a small group of Thomas langurs *(Presbytis thomasi)*. I was able to observe the monkeys only for a few precious minutes as they lingered in the lower branches of the tree.

It took several days waiting on a platform built at the top of a fig tree 30 metres above ground in Thailand's Khao Yai National Park before I got this shot of a lar or white-handed gibbon *(Hylobates lar)*. This lesser ape was really going out on a limb to enjoy some fresh figs.

At dawn in the rainforest regions of the Amazon basin you can hear the booming calls of red howler monkeys *(Alouatta seniculus)* marking their territories.

The flesh of woolly monkeys *(Lagothrix lagotricha)* is regarded as a delicacy by some native tribes in the Amazon. Young woolly monkeys are also kept as pets.

White-faced sakis *(Pithecia pithecia)* are related to capuchin monkeys and live in the rainforests of South America. Adult males have a distinctive white face and with a body weight of just two kilograms they are only slightly heavier than their female counterparts.

The pygmy marmoset *(Cebuella pygmaea)* is the smallest "true" monkey. Its body grows to a mere 15 centimetres and it feeds mainly on tree sap.

PAGE 222/223
As we flew over the Amazon basin I noticed a heart-shaped lake in the rainforest. The pilot had to bank heavily so I could take this photo through the open door.

The success of such a long-term project is only possible with the support of many people. For all their help in the field, at home and during the publication process, I would like to thank the following: Filippo Aureli, Richard Bodmer, Greg Cummings, Dhananjay Katjiu, Christoph Knogge, Francis Ndagijimana, Narendra Panwar and Edwin Sabuhoro. Without them I would not have been able to even find the beautiful monkeys and apes that we photographed in the wild. I would also of course like to thank my publishers, Monika Thaler and Gert Frederking; Ute Heek from Frederking & Thaler; Peter-Matthias Gaede, Ruth Eichhorn and Martin Meister from GEO; Christiane Breustedt from GEO International for their faith in me; Stefan Vogt for the design and layout; Karlheinz Rau for the production of the book; Frans de Waal for the foreword; Fritz Jantschke for the texts; and Lothar Frenz for his editorial work.

Special thanks go to my wife Silke Arndt who supported me with her professional advice as a graphic designer, ran the office during my trips, and kept contact with family and friends. She gave me the energy and the willpower necessary to make this book a reality.

Ingo Arndt, Langen